AF225727

SCIENCE TOOLS
I USE EVERYDAY

An Introduction to the Different Types of Tools
Used in Science Grade 1

Children's Books
on Science,
Nature & How
It Works

First Edition, 2024

Published in the United States by Speedy Publishing LLC, 40 E Main Street, Newark, Delaware 19711 USA.

© 2024 Baby Professor Books, an imprint of Speedy Publishing LLC

Baby Professor Books are available at special discounts when purchased in bulk for industrial and sales-promotional use. For details contact our Special Sales Team at Speedy Publishing LLC, 40 E Main Street, Newark, Delaware 19711 USA. Telephone (888) 248-4521 Fax: (210) 519-4043.

10 9 8 7 6 * 5 4 3 2 1

Print Edition: 9781541987197
Digital Edition: 9781541987586
Hardcover Edition: 9781541987975

See the world in pictures. Build your knowledge in style.
www.speedypublishing.com

TABLE OF CONTENTS

Have you ever asked questions about what you see? Why is the sky blue? What makes leaves fall? Believe it or not, asking questions is the first part of Science. Science is not just what you study in a book. Science is a method of learning. This book will teach you all about the Scientific method and tools you can use to practice Science.

Why is the sky blue?
What makes leaves fall?

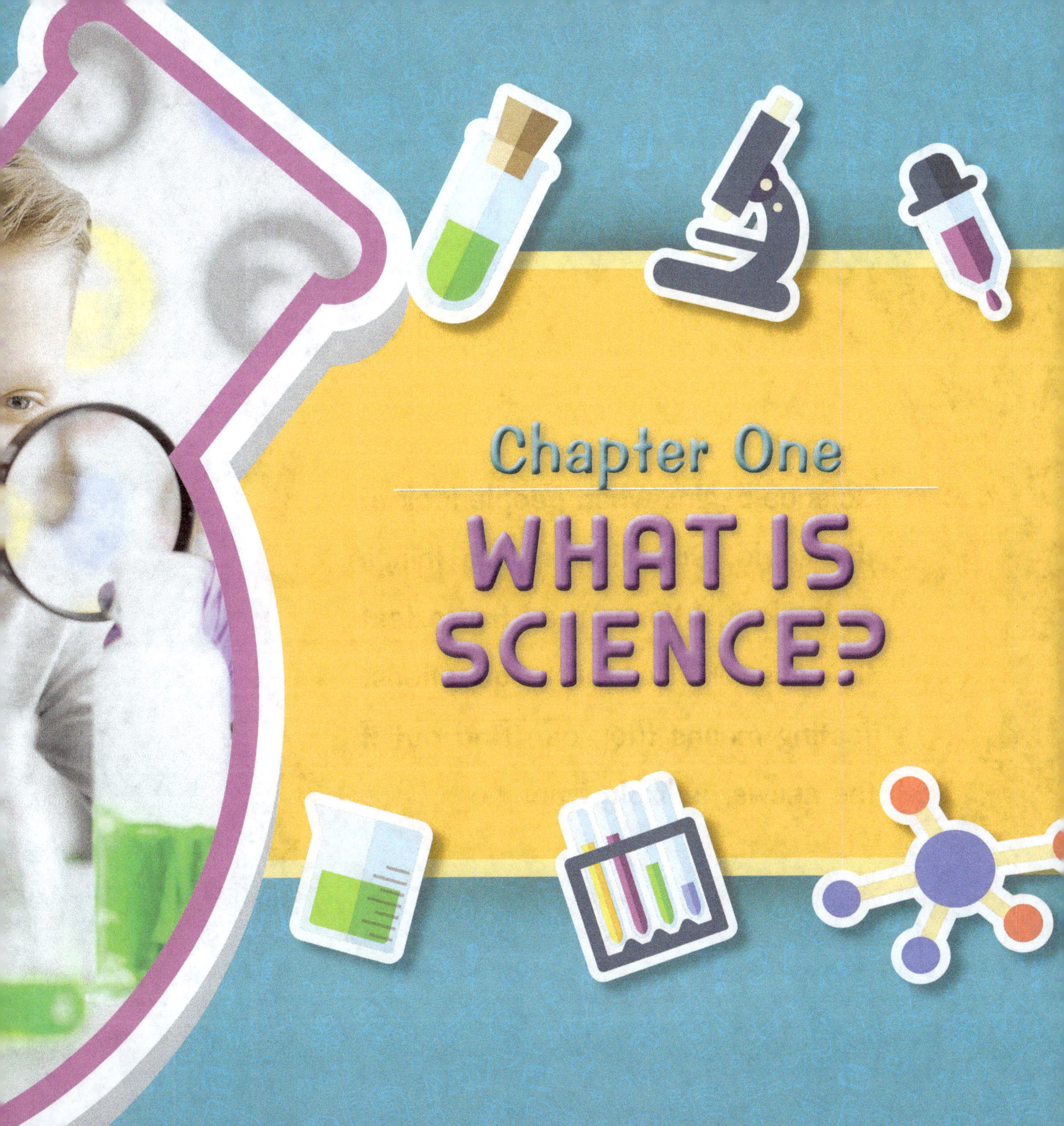

Chapter One

WHAT IS
SCIENCE?

Science begins when people look at the world. Scientists notice things and ask questions. They try to test the answers to these questions. Testing means they can find out if the answer is likely true.

Scientists collectively working on
a new generation experiment

HYPOT

For instance, a scientist might want to know if plants need water to grow. They guess that the answer is plants need water to grow. The scientific word for this answer is hypothesis. Science tests if that answer, or hypothesis, is true. Everything in Science has to be testable.

A hypothesis is an assumption that can be tested to see if it might be true.

DOING AN EXPERIMENT

These tests are called experiments. To find out if plants need water, you need to do a test. One way is to get two plants. Water one for a month and see if it grows. Do not water the other one for a month. Watch what happens. If the plant without water does not do well, plants probably need water.

Experimenting on two plants
with and without water

Lily
Cactus desert
14

Experiments are tricky. Some plants like cacti grow in the desert. They do not need much water. Imagine you do an experiment where you do not water the cactus. The other plant you use is a lily. You water the lily. The cactus does not need as much water as the lily. The cactus still does well.

Plants need water to survive.

You might think plants do not need water! This is not true. Scientists have to be very careful that everything in an experiment is the same. The only thing you change is the part you want to test.

Sometimes the hypothesis is wrong. That is not a bad thing in Science. You have still learned something. Scientists take notes about their observations during experiments. When the experiment is finished, they write a conclusion. This is their thoughts and results.

Scientists take notes about their observations during experiments.

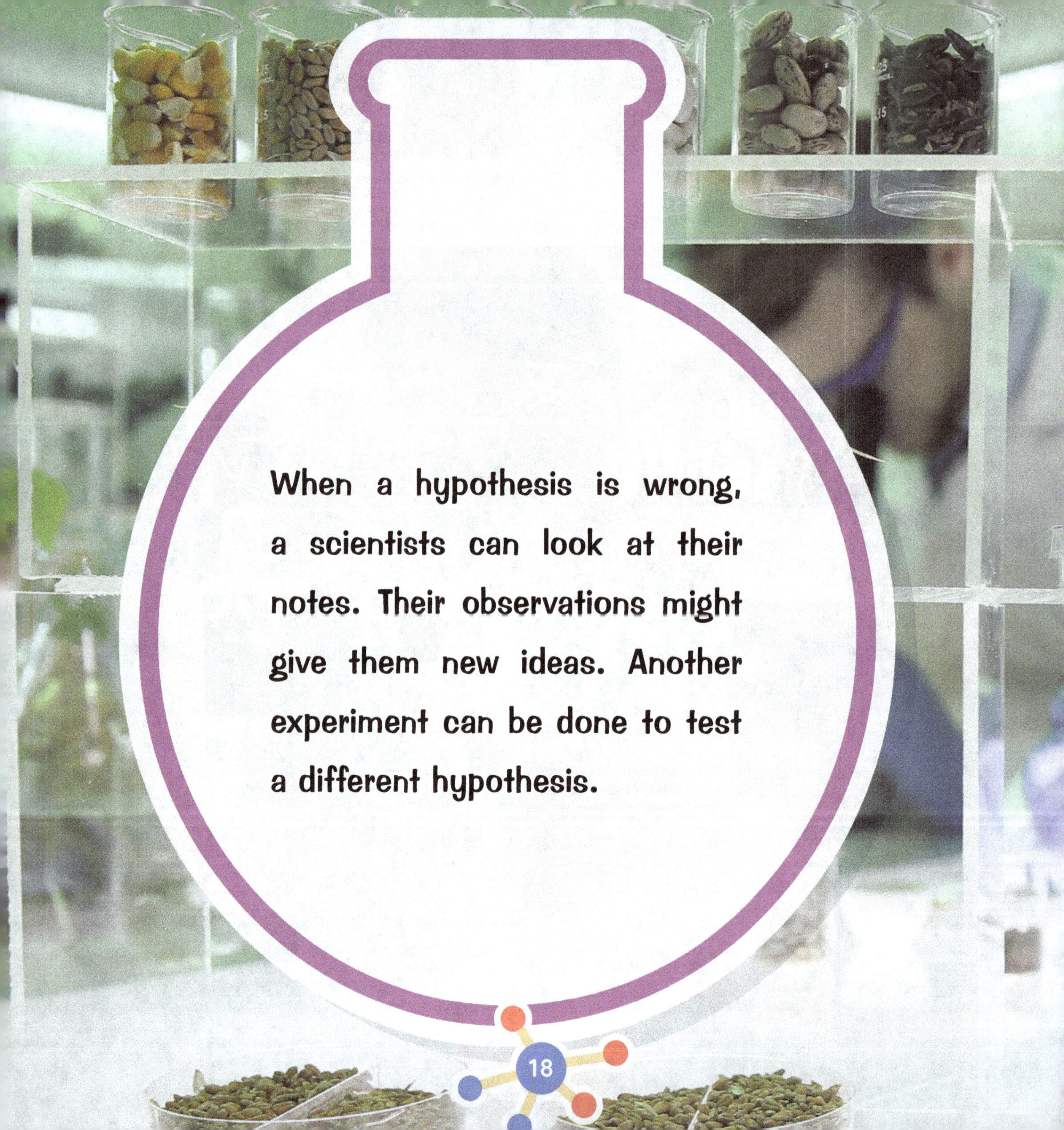
When a hypothesis is wrong, a scientists can look at their notes. Their observations might give them new ideas. Another experiment can be done to test a different hypothesis.

18

There is always room for more testing before something is completely proven. Write down the new hypothesis for future experiments.

In Science, all plants have scientific names. These names often come from an old language called Latin. These scientific names keep people from mixing up the wrong species of plants and animals. Mix-ups would be bad if someone else tries the same experiment. They might think the data was wrong!

Mulberry tree scientific name is Morus alba.
21

Scientists need to test many times to be certain their answers are correct.

REPEATING EXPERIMENTS

Imagine you have tested your plants. You have learned they need water to grow. That is not enough work to be a good scientist! Only two plants were tested. They were only tested once. Maybe they just got lucky. Scientists need to be certain their answers are correct. The only way to do this is to test many times. All science experiments should be repeatable by anyone. They should all have the same result. If the result is different, scientists need to find out why.

More experiments mean more evidence. Evidence is information that shows your hypothesis is probably right. Scientists record all this information. They can then share it with other scientists.

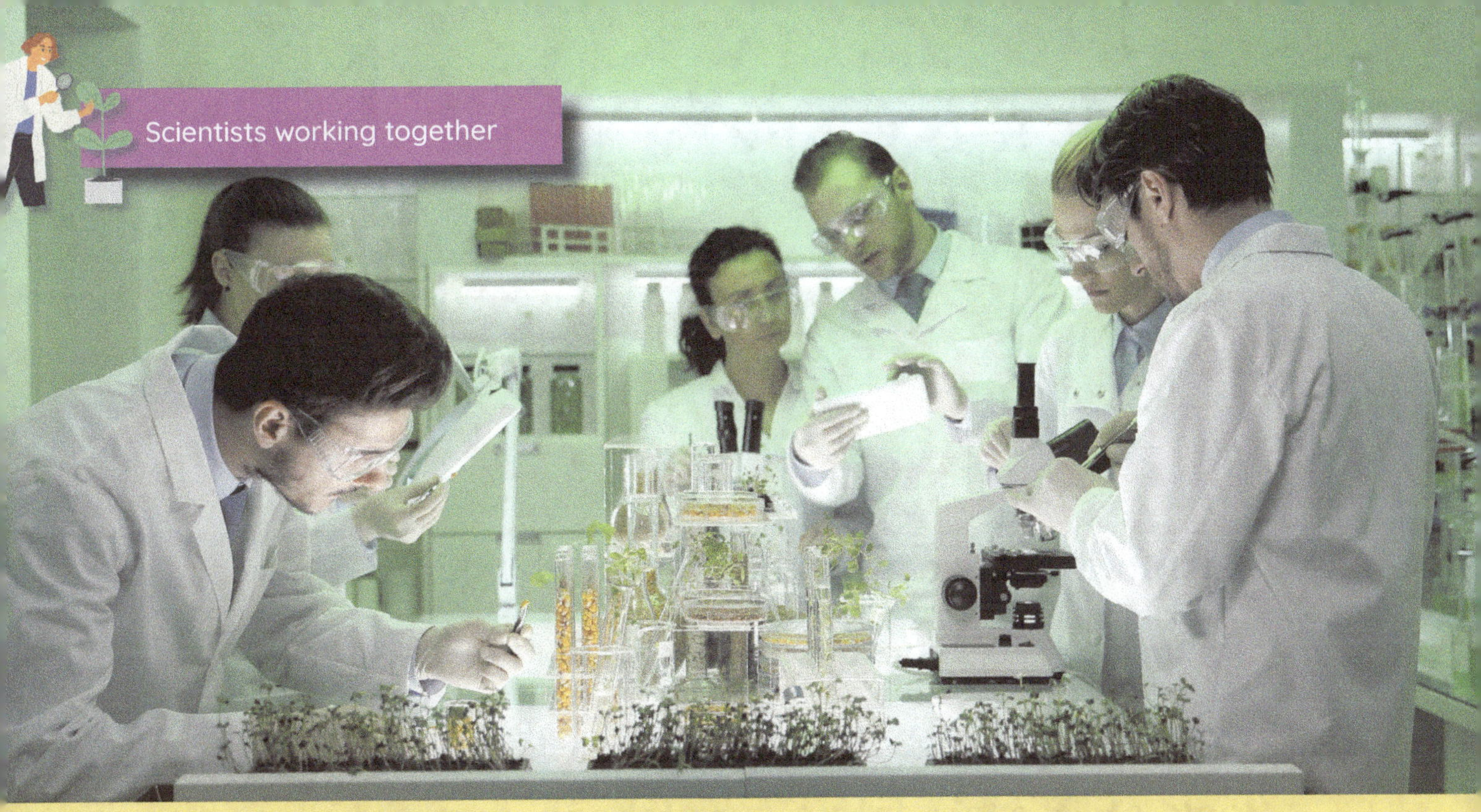

Scientists working together

Scientists can work together. They can check each other's work. They can find mistakes. New experiments are done to test new ideas. Sharing also means we can learn more. Scientists do not have to repeat all the work someone else did.

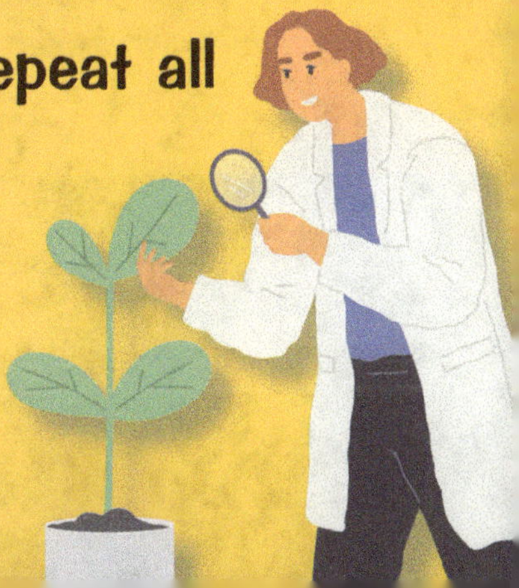

RECORDING RESULTS

Scientific tools can help us record things for other scientists. To record something in this case is to write down things you notice. That way you can look at it again later. A notebook and pencil are important tools. They help us write down what we observed. There are two main types of information or data: Qualitative and quantitative.

A notebook and a pencil are two important tools in Science.

Qualitative Research

Qualitative means you write down what you observed with your senses. What did you smell, feel, taste, hear, or see? What were the colors you saw change? Did you hear a popping sound when you did the experiment? All of these changes mean something happened. As scientists, we need to find out why.

Qualitative data refers to information you observed using your senses.

Quantitative means data that was measured. Quantitative data is useful because it is precise. People can easily test quantitative data.

It is harder to agree on qualitative data. Sometimes people see and hear things differently. It is still important though. All experiments begin with what we observe.

Quantitative data is precise data because it was measured.

When scientists record data, they often use things called graphs. They can make data easier to understand. There are many kinds of graphs. Bar graphs compare data. They show which group has more or less of something. Line graphs show how things are happening over time. Pie graphs show how much of things make up one whole.

Bar graph
Line graph
20%
Pie graph
33

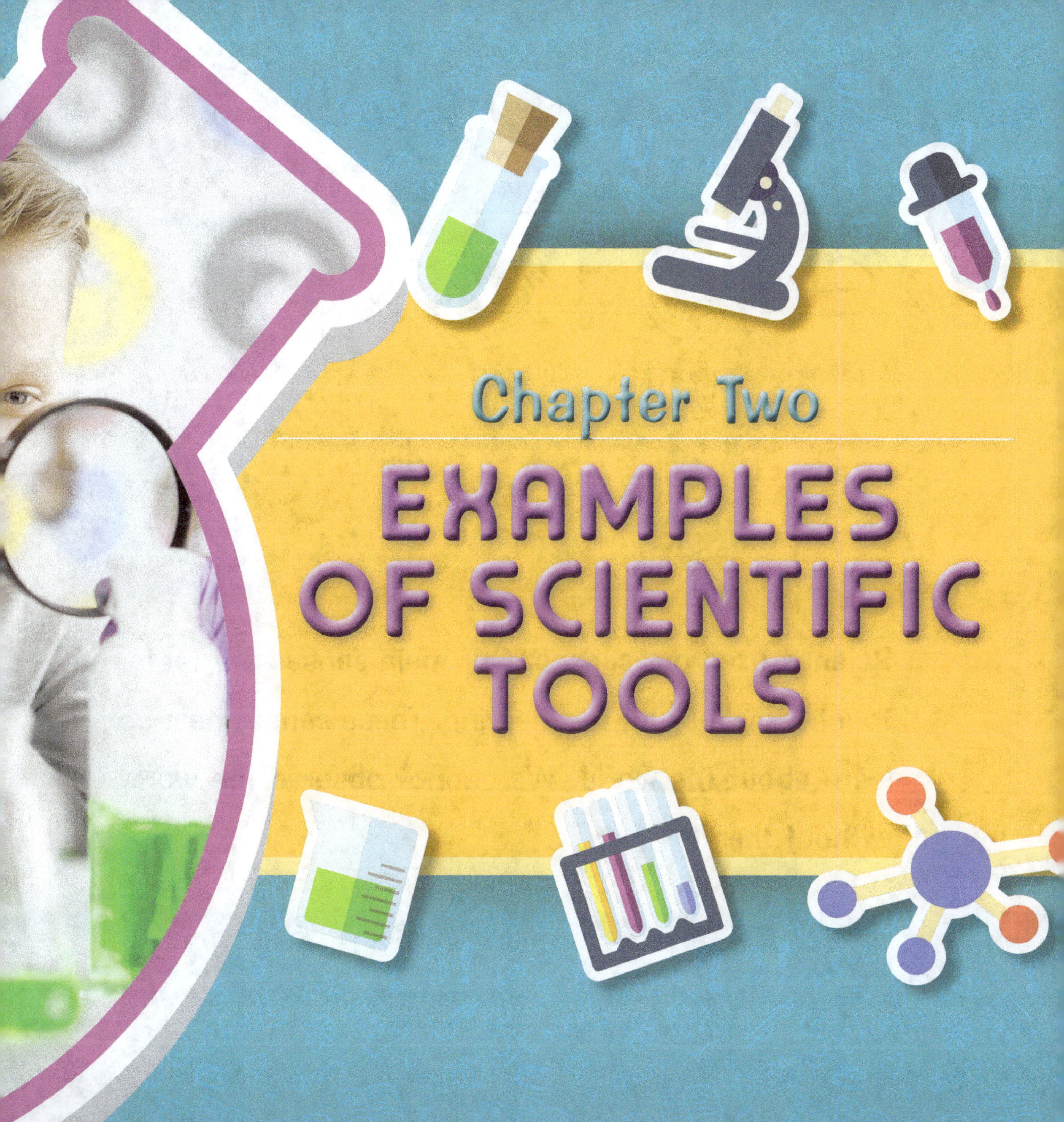
Chapter Two
EXAMPLES OF SCIENTIFIC TOOLS

5 SENSES

Science uses our senses. Our main senses are taste, touch, smell, sight, and hearing. These senses help us learn about the world. We cannot observe the world without them!

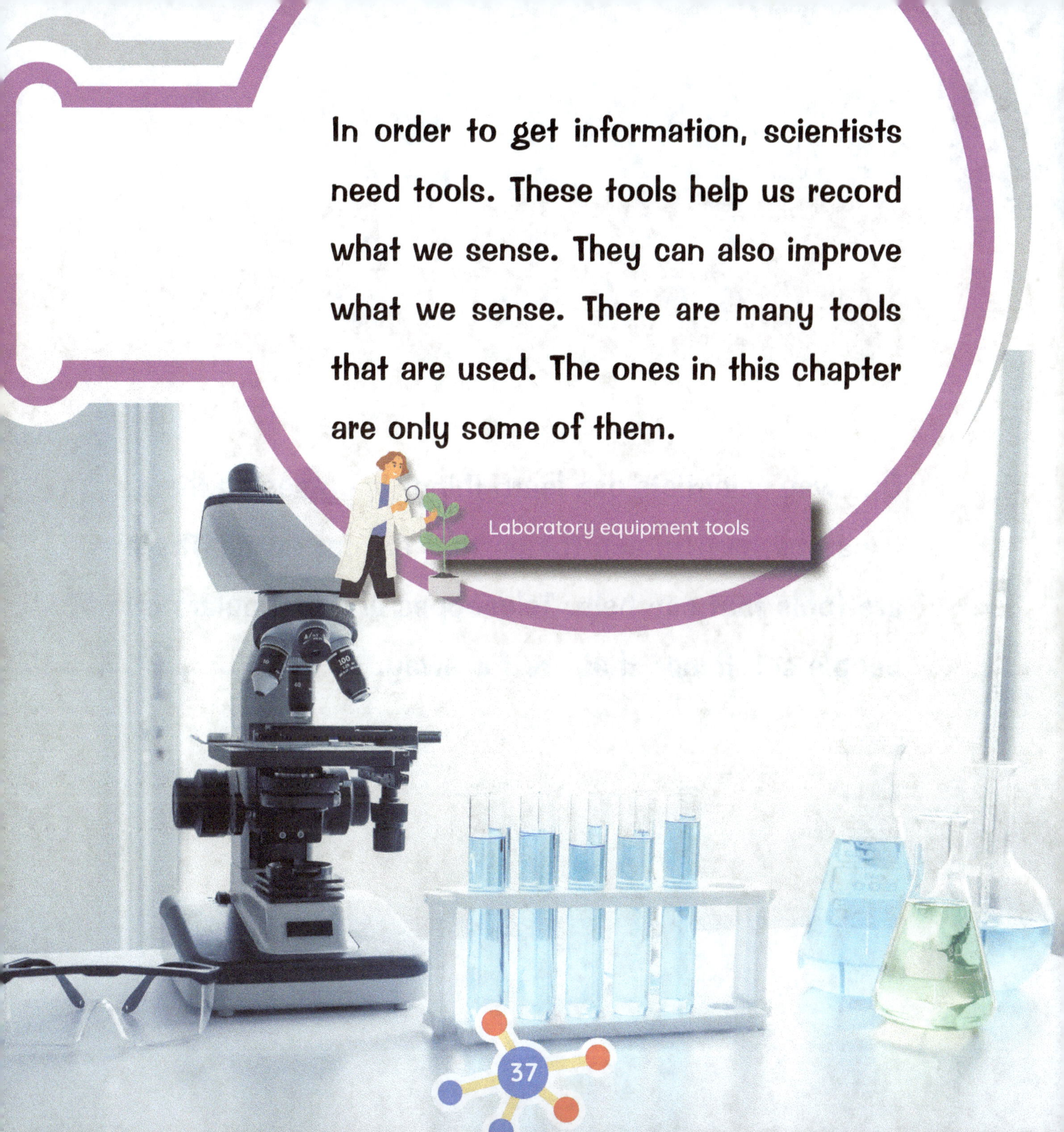

In order to get information, scientists need tools. These tools help us record what we sense. They can also improve what we sense. There are many tools that are used. The ones in this chapter are only some of them.

SEEING THINGS NEAR AND FAR

One way scientists can learn things is by seeing them. It can be hard to see things that are far away. There are tools that can help. Telescopes and binoculars let people see things that are far away.

A telescope and a binocular help scientists see things from far away.

Telescopes and binoculars have some differences. Telescopes are looked through with one eye. Binoculars are looked through with both eyes. Telescopes are larger and bigger than binoculars. Binoculars are easier to carry. Telescopes are better for seeing things in the dark. Binoculars need more light. Often telescopes are used for seeing things in the night sky. Binoculars are used for seeing things on land.

Telescopes are better for seeing things in the dark
Binoculars are looked through both eyes
41

It is hard for people to see things that are really small. Magnifying glasses and microscopes can help. A magnifying glass is also called a hand lens. It is called that because you can hold it in one hand. Magnifying glasses are easy to carry around. They cannot make things look as big as microscopes do though.

Magnifying glass

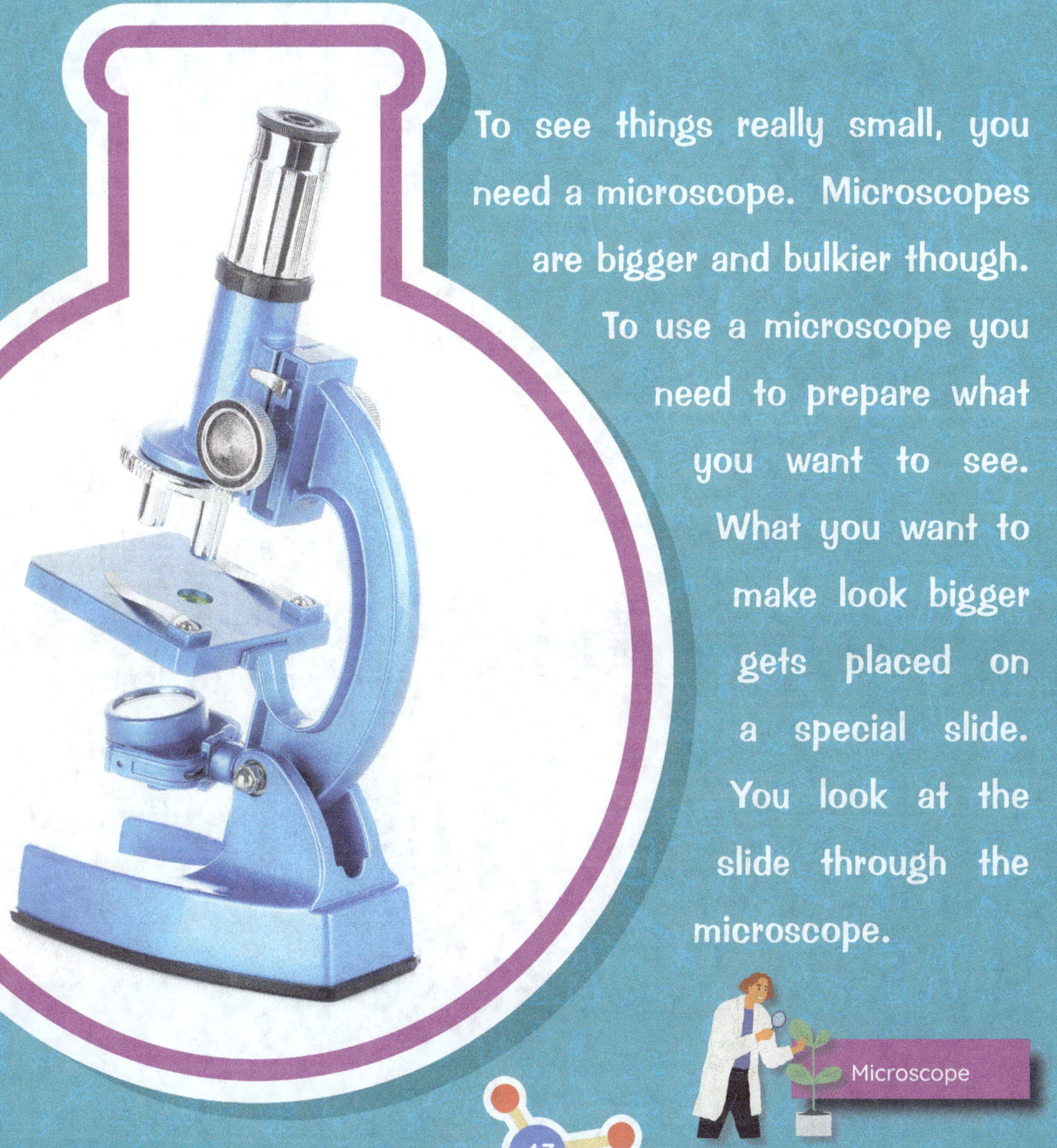

To see things really small, you need a microscope. Microscopes are bigger and bulkier though. To use a microscope you need to prepare what you want to see. What you want to make look bigger gets placed on a special slide. You look at the slide through the microscope.

A digital camera is also a useful tool. Taking a picture means we can look and study things more closely. This is helpful if what we want to learn can only be seen every so often.

Digital camera

Telescopes, magnifying glasses, and binoculars all make things bigger because they bend light! They use glass or plastic lenses to do this. This same idea is why people can use glasses to see well. The light goes through the lenses in a special way. This affects the way our eyes see things.

Balancing scale
balance
2 kg - 5 lb
CAPACITY

MEASURING MASS AND VOLUME

Mass is how much of something there is. It is measured using weighing scales. There are many kinds of weighing scales. The best kind to understand mass is the balance scale. This kind of scale works by finding which weights balance.

On one side of the scale you put on a weight that you know the mass of. On the other side, you put the things you want to know the mass of. If the unknown object is heavier than the weights on the other side, the balance dips down. To find out what the proper mass is, take some weights off the other side. When the balance is perfectly balanced, both objects have the same mass. Add up the weights on the side you know and it will be the same mass on the other side. It is a bit like being on a see-saw. Mass is measured in grams.

A doctor is weighing the medicines by a balance scale at the laboratory

Other weighing scales are simpler. If you have ever stepped on a scale to get your weight in kilograms, you have used a weighing scale. These kinds of scales depend on Earth's gravity to work.

When gravity pulls people down, it gives them weight. The more mass you have, the more you weigh. A weighing scale would not be correct on the moon. There is less gravity there.

The more mass a person has, the more the person weighs.

On the moon you would weigh less! A balancing scale would work on the moon though. This is because it can help detect if the mass of things is the same even if gravity changes.

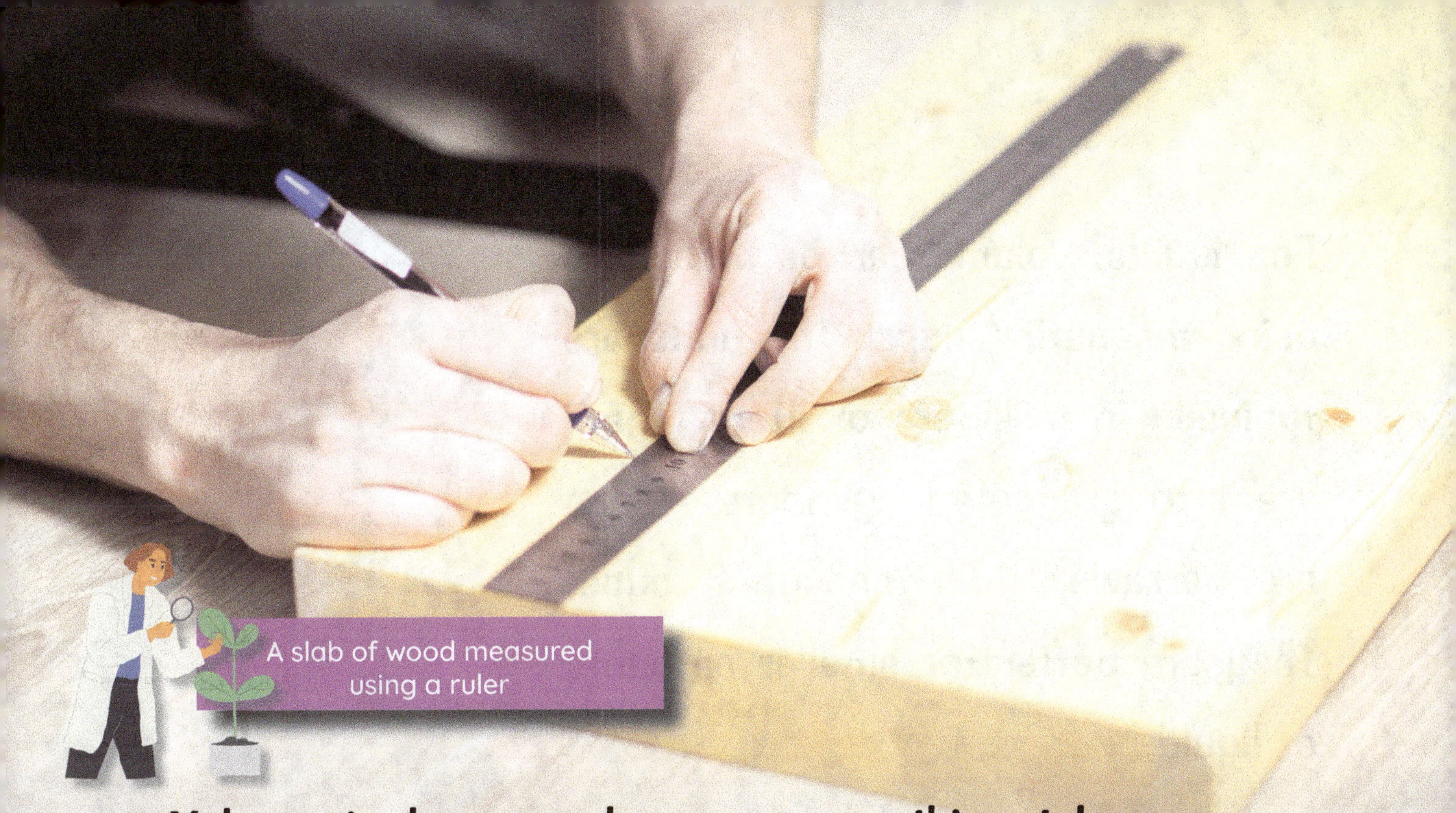

A slab of wood measured using a ruler

Volume is how much space something takes up. For solids, it can be measured using rulers or tape measures. The units of measurement are often centimeters or millimeters. These tools measure height, how long something is from top to bottom. They also measure width. That is how long something is straight across.

For liquids, volume can be measured using measuring cups. The units are typically in milliliters or liters. There are also graduated cylinders. These are narrower than measuring cups. They are better for smaller amounts of liquid.

A measuring cup and graduated cylinder

Beakers are a tool used by scientists. They hold liquids. Beakers often have lines on the side. These lines help measure the volume of liquid. They are not as precise as measuring cups or graduated cylinders.

There are other units of measurement. Sometimes people measure mass in pounds or length in inches. The measurement system that uses grams and meters is called the Metric System. The Metric System is the number one system for Science. Having everyone use the same measurements makes it easier to share data.

Metric Units

kilo	hecto	deca	unit	deci	centi	milli
kilometer	hectometer	decameter	meter	decimeter	centimeter	millimeter
kilogram	hectogram	decagram	gram	decigram	centigram	milligram
kiloliter	hectoliter	decaliter	liter	deciliter	centiliter	milliliter

OTHER USEFUL TOOLS

Other interesting things to measure can be the temperature, acidity, time, or magnetism. A thermometer is used to measure temperature. Thermometers have a special liquid inside. The hotter it gets, the higher the liquid rises on the scale. You can look at the top of the liquid and see what number goes with it. This is how hot or cold it is. Temperature is measured in degrees of Fahrenheit or Celsius.

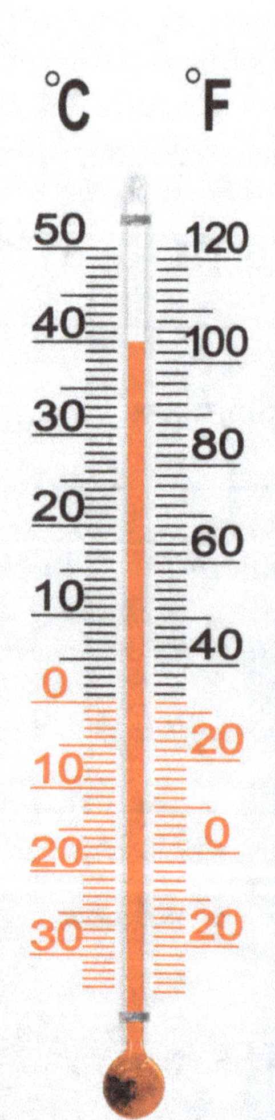

A concept of thermometers in hot and cold weather.

Acidity is caused by the make-up of matter. If something is acidic enough, it can melt things! Not all acids are dangerous though. Some acids you can eat. Vinegar is an acid. Acids are bitter.

Vinegar is an example of acid you can eat.

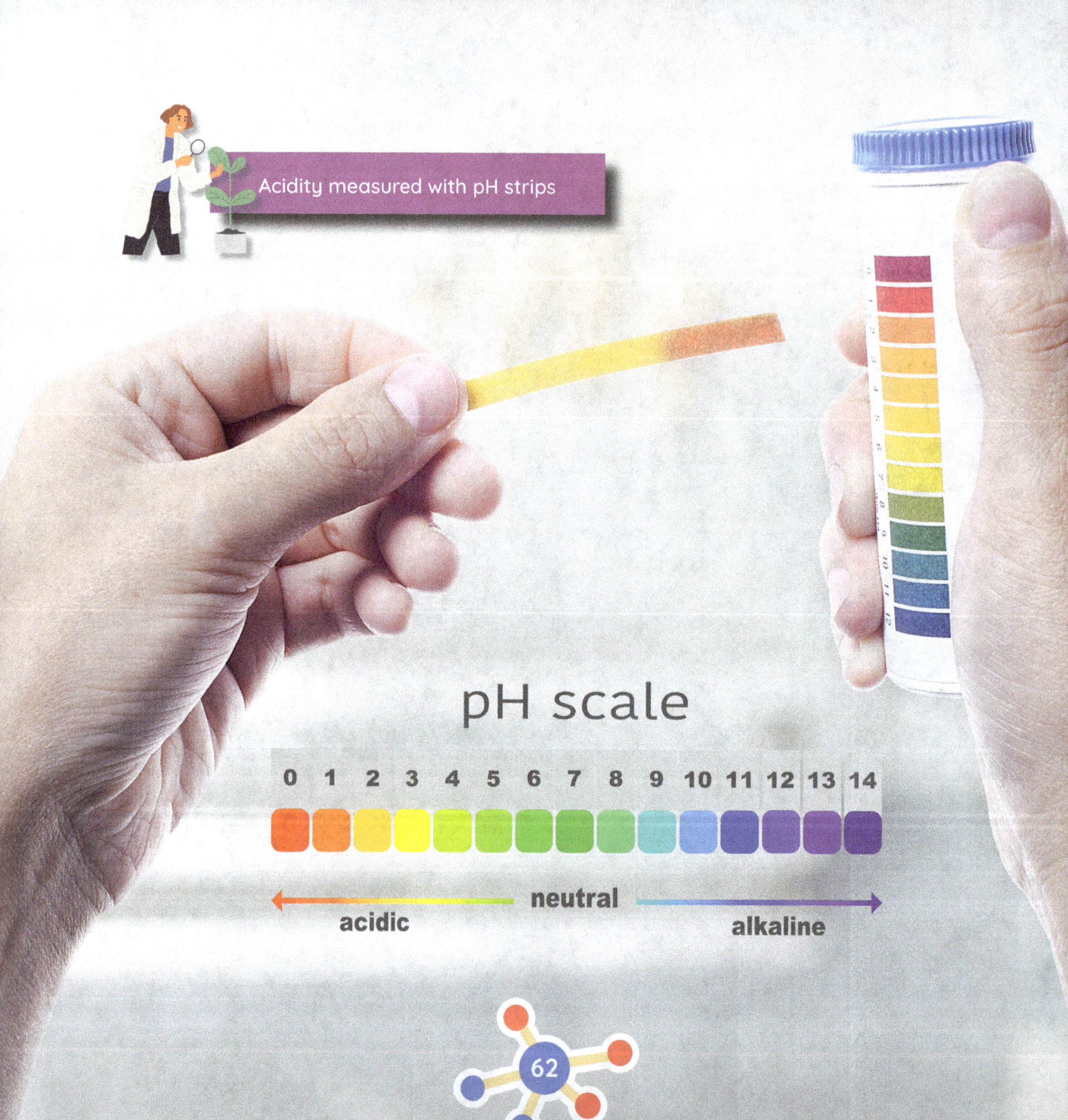

Acidity measured with pH strips
pH scale
0 1 2 3 4 5 6 7 8 9 10 11 12 13 14
neutral
acidic
alkaline
62

Acidity can be measured with pH strips. If you put a pH test strip in a liquid, it will usually change color. If the liquid is neutral, it will stay a yellowish-green color. The more acidic it is, the redder it will get. The more alkaline, the darker purple it will get. Alkaline is the opposite of acidic. It is also called basic. The pH scale goes from 0-14. The closer to zero the more acidic the liquid is, and the closer to fourteen, the more alkaline. A seven is neutral.

Stopwatches can be used to measure time. If you want to know how quickly something happens, this is a good tool to use. You can simply hit a button when you begin your experiment. Then hit the stop button when it is done. Then you will know how long your experiment took to do.

Stopwatch

65

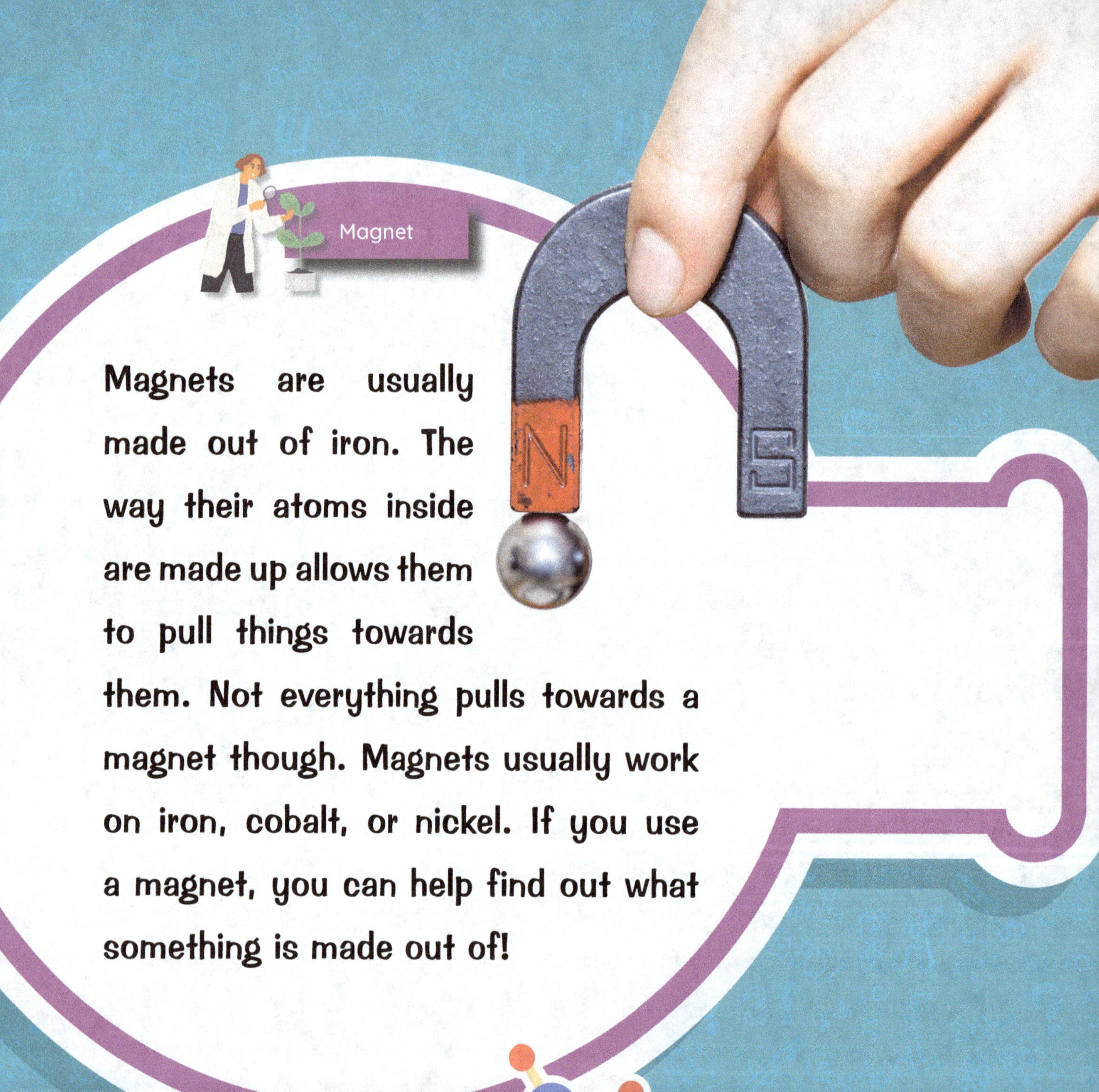

Magnets are usually made out of iron. The way their atoms inside are made up allows them to pull things towards them. Not everything pulls towards a magnet though. Magnets usually work on iron, cobalt, or nickel. If you use a magnet, you can help find out what something is made out of!

SAFETY AND EASE

Not all tools used in Science are for measuring things. It is also important to be safe. Scientists sometimes use special glasses. This prevents anything dangerous getting into their eyes. They might use gloves to protect their hands. When doing an experiment, it is important to make certain that you are safe.

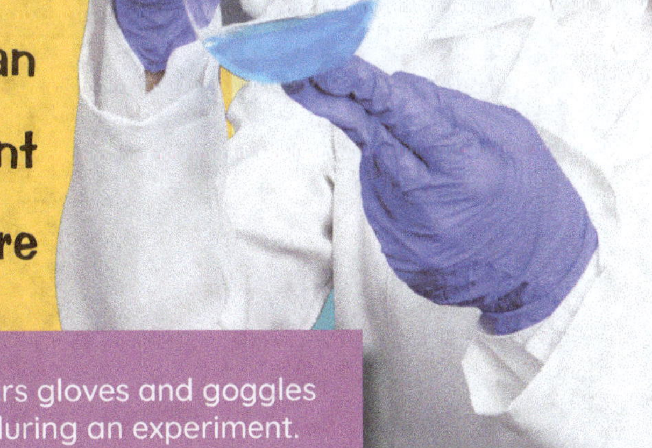

A scientist wears gloves and goggles to stay safe during an experiment.

Nets are one of the tools
that scientists need

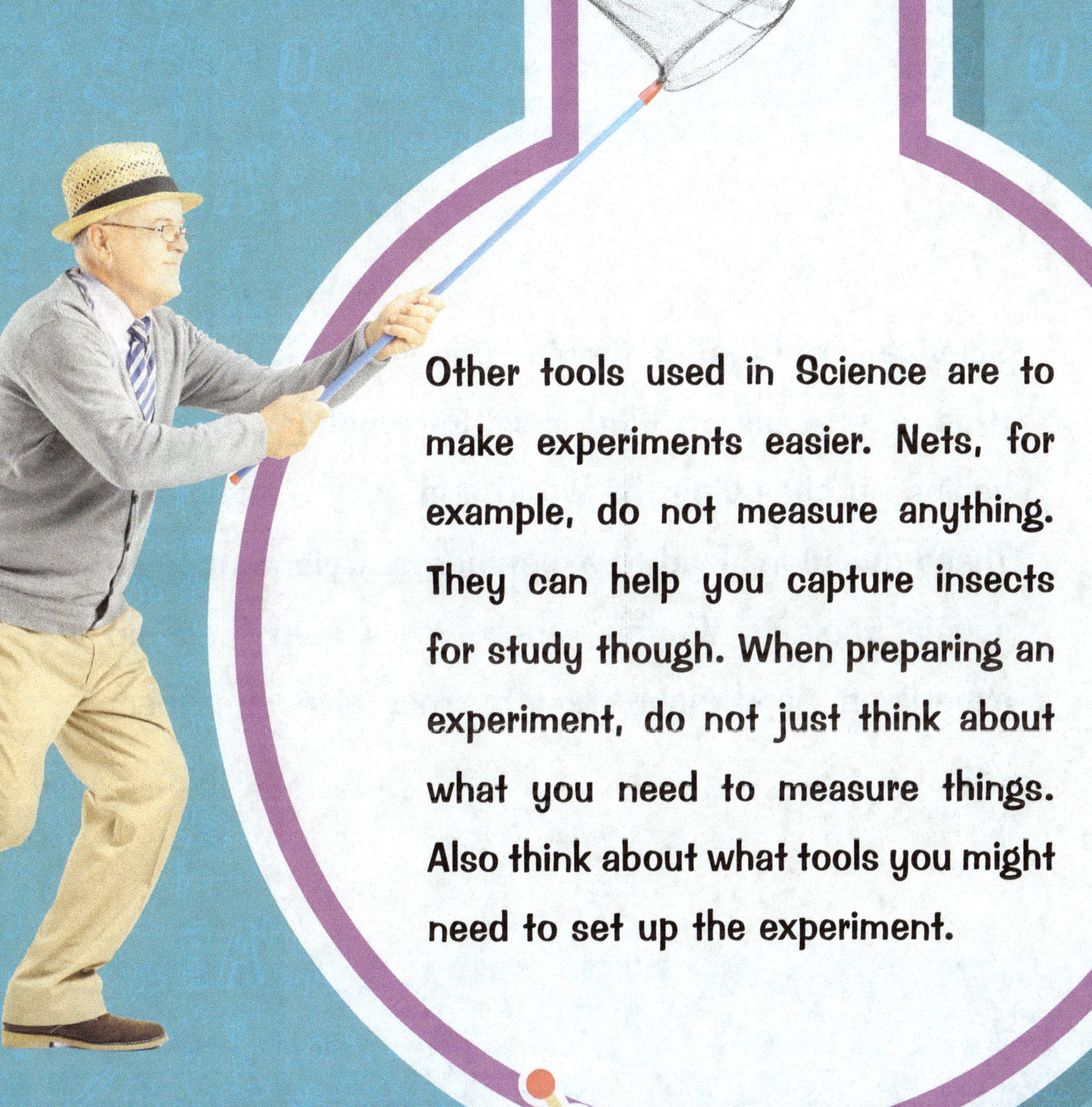

Other tools used in Science are to make experiments easier. Nets, for example, do not measure anything. They can help you capture insects for study though. When preparing an experiment, do not just think about what you need to measure things. Also think about what tools you might need to set up the experiment.

Science is not just something you learn from a book. It is a process to find new information. Science begins by observing the world and asking questions. These questions lead to experiments. Scientists need special tools to do this. These tools help them do experiments and record results. They also keep them safe.

Visit

www.speedypublishing.com

To view and download free content on your favorite subject and browse our catalog of new and exciting books for readers of all ages.